Australians
and
North Americans

InterAct 2

George W. Renwick

Intercultural Press, Inc.

Library of Congress Catalogue Card Number 80-83910
ISBN 0-933662-16-5

Copyright © 1980 by Intercultural Press, Inc.

Printed in the United States of America

Published by Intercultural Press, Inc.
P.O. Box 768
Yarmouth, Maine 04096

(207) 846-5168

"I find the rhythms different here. It's almost a curse we have the same language. It deludes us about you guys and you about us. We're as different from Americans and the British as we are the French. I've often thought we ought to subtitle our pictures."

Fred Schepsi
Australian Film Director
on location in the U.S.
December 25, 1980

TABLE OF CONTENTS

FOREWORD

Our purpose at the Intercultural Press in publishing this
volume is to enable Americans and Australians who are or will
be working together to approach their relationships and
assignments with greater confidence and to accomplish their
objectives--personal, family, and professional--more completely.

Confidence and effectiveness cannot be gained through
reading descriptions of life in Australia or the United States
(culture-specific studies), although these provide helpful
information. Nor can intercultural competence be gained
through comparisons of the U.S. and Australia
(culture-comparative studies), though these too offer valuable
background.

What men and women working with people from other culture
groups need most are practical guidelines on what to do, and
what not to do, when. They must be able to make decisions,
evaluate their own responses and those of others, and account
for what happens when people from different cultural
backgrounds interact on a day-to-day basis.

A culture interactive study like this one probes, explains,
and predicts what happens when individuals who have grown up in
different cultures meet, eat, joke, argue, fight, and cooperate
with one another. Such a study makes clear what each person
must do in order to become a clever competitor or a trusted
colleague and friend.

This volume, therefore, and the other volumes in this series, explain how people from one culture see those in another; what exactly they expect from each other; how they effect each other when they are together; and how what is said and done by one embarrasses, frustrates, motivates, impresses, and angers the other.

Many American and Australian businesspeople and members of their families have been involved in the preparation of this study. They provided information when the study was in process and recommendations on the preparation of the manuscript when it was reported. We are indebted to them for their assistance. The material in this volume has appeared in other forms. A series of articles based on the study ran in Australian Financial Review. An earlier version of the work has been used extensively in preparing Americans and Australians to work effectively together in multinational corporations.

1. INTRODUCTION

Australians and Americans have usually had rather high regard for one another--as long as they were some distance apart. It would seem these two peoples should be able to get along right well together. Often, however, they cannot. They expect a lot of one another, but their expectations are frequently frustrated. Both are surprised to find chronic tension between them and a real ambivalence in their feelings about one another. Even severe conflicts sometimes erupt.

There are several reasons why Australians and Americans experience difficulties with one another:

- When two people share some basic similarities, their differences usually stand out; instead of being interesting, their differences are irritating. Basic similarities, together with pronounced differences, often produce more misunderstanding and conflict than do on similarities at all.

● What determines the level of tension and conflict between two peoples is not how many points they differ on, but which points. If the points on which two peoples differ the most are not salient to either, there will be little conflict. If the points of greatest contrast happen to be very salient to one or another of the peoples, however, even if the number of such points is few, they may go to war. (This is the primary reason why domestic strife and civil wars are sometimes the most vicious and most devastating; the differences, though few, matter.) There may be only one point on which the parties differ, but if it is tied to beliefs and feelings which are deep, the conflict will be severe. Americans and Australians, despite their similarities, happen to differ on certain points, each of which is highly significant to one or the other.

● Perhaps most importantly, when two peoples expect to encounter differences in one another (as, for example, do Americans and Japanese), their discovery of a point on which they are similar is exciting and reassuring. When two peoples each expect the other to be much like themselves (as do Australians and Americans), and then encounter a striking difference, they are taken aback and confused. When difference then follows upon unexpected difference, it can easily become irritating. Chronic aggravation results when the disruptive differences are felt but not specifically located, labeled and dealt with.

The sources of their differences can usually be traced to general characteristics which many Australians have and to general characteristics which many Americans have. These, in turn, can be traced to the distinctive cultures in which Australians and Americans have grown up and within which they are used to living and working.

The purpose of this study is to analyze the two cultures, identify points of basic similarity and significant difference, describe the corresponding characteristics of each of the peoples and locate some of the particular difficulties between them.

An understanding of the social and professional relations between Australians and Americans requires more, however, than analysis of their respective cultures and the similarities and differences between them. It requires consideration of the interaction itself, the direct effect of each upon the other. Many people feel that an Australian is an Australian no matter what the situation, and that an American is always an American. To some extent their basic characteristics do carry over from one situation and relationship to the next. Such an interpretation, however, is an individualistic (primary Western) one, where each individual is seen as autonomous and quite unaffected by particular situations and interactions; a limited and only partially accurate interpretation.

Often the behavior of a person is the result of the other person with whom he or she is interacting, the result of their particular relationship (and the interplay of their differing backgrounds and distinctive cultural characteristics). An American, therefore, may think, feel and do things with an Australian that he or she probably would not with someone, say, from Japan. Interaction with an Australian may generate perceptions and evoke responses which interaction with someone from another culture would not. More specifically, Australians and Americans often evoke from one another exactly that behavior which reinforces their images of one another. Their images are often not very complimentary; they become even less complimentary as the interaction progresses. In this study, therefore, we will suggest specific things an American can do when with an Australian, and certain things that would harm the relationship, in order to ensure that their mutual perceptions and reactions are as positive as possible.

In light of the above, the first questions to be asked are, "What do Australians expect and feel? How do they behave? Why?" The next and more productive question is, "What do Australians feel and how do they behave when they are with Americans in America?' Then follows the question, "What then should Americans do?" This study will deal with all of these questions.

There is a further question, however, and discussions which explore this one are the most productive: "What do the Australians feel, what do they expect, how do they behave, and what should the Americans do in a given situation in a given organization?" This question is best dealt with by the particular Americans and Australians involved.

In particular characteristics of the cultures and the patterns of perception, behavior and interaction described below are consistently expressed in, and reinforced by, many aspects of each culture (the structure of organizations and governments, social customs, art and literature, religious beliefs, etc.). These will not be included in here. They are also expressed in, and reinforced by, firmly established patterns of non-verbal behavior (gestures, intonation, personal space, etc.). Although central to interaction between Australians and Americans, these particular non-verbal patterns of behavior have not been investigated and therefore will not be included in this study.

While reading the analysis which follows, it is important to bear in mind that the descriptions of Australians and Americans are generalizations. The basic characteristics described, of course, are not found in every Australian or every American. Certainly, they are not found to the same degree in each person. What is described are the backgrounds and some of the basic qualities which many Australians share to some extent with other Australians, and some of the basic qualities which many Americans share to some extent with other Americans. What is also suggested in the following is what happens sometimes, perhaps frequently--but not always--when Australians and Americans, having derived some of their basic qualities from dissimilar groups, spend time with one another in social and business settings.

Cultures, of course, shape the values and behavior of both the men and women within them. Within a particular culture, however, the influences upon the men are usually somewhat different from those of the women. The qualities of Australians and Americans described below, although they often characterize both the men and the women in each culture, sometimes are more characteristic of the men.

At various points in this study, the perceptions which Australians and Americans have of each other are presented. (Americans, for example, tend to see Australians as arrogant. Australians, on the other hand, tend to see Americans as boring.) These mutual perceptions, which are often rather negative, are not presented as an indictment of either people; this is simply the way these two peoples, at this point in the evolution of their cultures and their relations with one another, see each other.

If the reader, after reading this study, sees both Australians and Americans in rather negative terms, he is experiencing the same perceptions which these two peoples actually have of one another. We hope, instead, that the reader--unlike most Americans and Australians today--will anticipate certain differences, recognize them immediately when they are disruptive, and be able to take advantage of the differences as well as the similarities between these two complex, intriguing peoples.

2. SIMILARITIES

The fundamental ideas and institutions of both Australia and America have been transplanted from other countries, primarily the British Isles, during the past few hundred years. The peoples, too, have been transplanted. Both Australia and America are nations of immigrants. We are dealing, therefore, with two peoples whose origins and basic characteristics are Anglo-Saxon and whose social and political orientations are democratic.

Because of their common heritage, most Australians and Americans have the same language, the same religion, and the same skin color, and they are similar in their ways of greeting, eating, drinking, and dressing.

Conscious of the fact that their cultures are derivative, Australians and Americans have worked at developing distinctive national identities of their own. Both have therefore shown special respect for individuals most thoroughly molded by indigenous influences and least susceptible to European ones.

Essential to their identities is the fact that both peoples share a similar, prolonged experience within their own countries: the challenge, hardship and appeal of vast unexplored, undeveloped territories--a frontier. Their experiences on their remote frontiers, and the popular and still influential legends from the frontiers, have contributed to other basic qualities which Australians and Americans share; both peoples are practical, inventive, good at improvisation, and both place relatively low value on intellectual and spiritual pursuits. Australians and Americans are adaptable, direct and forthright in their manner and very informal. They are also gregarious; Australians living in the United States, for example, usually know quite a few of their neighbors and they frequently have Americans into their homes.

Like most Australians, in fact like most nationalities, Americans are quite ethnocentric. They assume that their own beliefs and ways of doing things are better than the available alternatives. Their approach to, and evaluation of, other peoples reveal these assumptions. Any challenge to their assumptions is not regarded kindly.

Like most Americans, the Australians are very mobile. They migrate freely and frequently from state to state.

Both Americans and Australians are now accustomed to living in highly industrialized and thoroughly urban environments. Both are conscious of, and proud of, being modern. Because such environments and values shape similar life styles, most Australians find that living in the United States is close to what they expected it to be.

Given this common heritage, these similar environments and experiences, and these similar personal characteristics, Australians and Americans usually assume more similarity between them, more understanding and agreement, than actually exist. Despite their common origins and their resemblance to one another now, there are important differences between their societies and cultures, and therefore between their values, priorities, attitudes, motivations, and modes of interaction. Some of these differences will be described in the following chapters.

3. DIFFERENCES

<u>THE LAND</u>

The differences between Australians and Americans begin with the landscapes in which they grew up and with which, to varying degrees, they identify. Australians are accustomed to uniformity in their landscape and in the land itself. They live with, and are influenced by, a sameness in their desert inland and the only comparatively less dry coastal areas. Their attitudes toward themselves and others have been shaped by their adaptation to this dry land.

Americans, on the other hand, are familiar with climate and topography which contrast sharply from one region to

another. Many Americans have learned to adapt to their
differing environments and to enjoy and take advantage of them.
When Americans sing (which they rarely do now), they sometimes
express with some pride the diversity of their land.

SOCIAL STRUCTURE

Differences between Australians and Americans are also to
be found in the populations of which they are a part. The
differences in the size of the population is striking:
Australia now has about 15 million people whereas the United
States has more than 200 million.

More important are the differences in the composition of
the populations. Both Australians and Americans have
experienced the assimilation of substantial numbers of
foreigners. The countries from which the immigrants came to
Australia, however, were fewer, and the cultures from which
they came were more similar, than were the countries and
cultures from which the immigrants came to the United States.
Partly because of the White Australia Policy, the total
non-European population of Australia is less than one percent.
The subcultures and races of Australia are therefore very
homogeneous (with the exception, of course, of the Aboriginal
tribes).

The cultures and races of the United States, on the other
hand, having originated not only in Europe but in Africa, Asia,
Russia, and Latin America as well, are still easily
distinguished from one another. Americans, therefore, live
with not only marked regional differences, but with cultural
and racial differences as well.

The social classes in Australia are also unusually homogeneous, more so than in the United States. Most of the early immigrants to Australia were from a single class (the lower class), and the process of migration itself reduced distinctions between classes and reduced the traditional respect for social rank. The result has been the firm belief, shared by most Australians, that "Jack's as good as his master." This belief is manifest in numerous aspects of Australian culture. Australians are, for example, extremely informal in their rendering and receiving of personal services. Specific examples would include the taxi driver's expectation that a single passenger would get in beside him, and the fact that offering a tip for personal service often gives offense.

There are differences, too, in attitudes toward manual labor. For Australians, no shame is attached to performing manual labor and lower status is not implied in doing so. For Americans, however, occupations involving manual labor are not as respected as those requiring _mental_ labor. Because they see one's status as being derived from one's occupation, Americans have less respect for those who do manual labor.

Because of their _lack_ of _class_ _distinctions_ and social rank, one can approach most Australians, no matter how high their position, with the certainty of an attentive, cordial hearing. This is often not the case in the United States. One is more likely to approach an American of high position with some reticence, some sense of imposition, some awareness of the other demands upon the person's time, if indeed one can gain access to the person in the first place.

Because, in part, of the homogeneity of their social structure, there is little physical violence in the lives and cultures of the Australians. In America culture, however, physical and other forms of violence are pervasive and increasing, a situation which causes considerable concern for many overseas visitors, including Australians, while they are in the United States.

In spite of the fact that the differences between their classes are small, and the tone of their society is generally democratic, the Australians have a high degree of class-consciousness, a higher degree than do Americans. One instance where their class-consciousness was clearly evident is described by Dr. C. W. Bean, an eminent Australian historian. The situation involved Australian diggers (soldiers) during the First World War:

> In Australia the distinction into social classes was so resented that it was difficult to get born Australians to serve as officers' batmen and grooms, who by the English tradition were servants. . . .

The acute class-consciousness of many Australians continues today and they bring it with them when they come to the United States. They are, therefore, often curious about the more distinctive classes in the United States but often show little tolerance for them and little flexibility in adjusting to them. For the same reasons, Australians come to the United States ready to resist being categorized or classified themselves and to resist being treated differently, especially when they perceive the classification to be lower and the treatment to be condescending.

SOCIAL RELATIONS

Cooperation and Competition

Given the relatively recent frontier experience which Australians share, and given the small differences between their subcultures, classes, and races and the small gap between rich and poor, most Australians have a strong sense of community. They therefore tend to value collective effort highly, more highly than do Americans. Rugged individualism, a formative traditional value for Americans, is less respected by Australians. As a consequence, collectivist or socialist ideas and "paternalistic" legislation are more widespread in Australia than in the United States.

Because of these differences in experience and values, an Australian begins interaction with an American on the basis of a more collectivist, cooperative orientation; the American begins on the basis of a more individualistic, competitive orientation.

Mates vs. Friends

One of the central areas in which Australians and Americans differ is in their experience of, and attitude toward, friendship. Each brings different expectations to a potential friendship. The chances of misunderstanding are therefore rather high, as are the chances for feeling of rejection and resentment.

In order to locate the sources of these differences, it is important to look once again at the circumstances in which

Australians and Americans found themselves as they began building their nations. Conditions confronting the first European settlers in Australia were very harsh. Consequently the settlers, most of them convicts, developed among themselves a sense of mutual dependence. This sense was conveyed to subsequent generations and was nourished throughout Australian colonial history by similar circumstances and necessities. The people, for example, lacked doctors, hospitals, and other facilities and had to rely upon each other. Although many of the circumstances have changed now, this pattern of interdependence has persisted.

In contrast to the Australians, the early Americans, when confronted with their own circumstances which were equally adverse in some ways, looked to themselves and emphasized self-reliance, or to a relatively small group with which they were in frequent, immediate contact. These independent (and often idiosyncratic) individuals and these distinct groups then became contentious factions when decisions affecting all of them had to be made. With some modifications, this pattern has persisted.

Emerging from their particular heritage are the Australians' fundamental beliefs that one has a responsibility for his or her neighbor and that loyalty to one's friends is not only appropriate, it is essential. An Australian assumes a natural, basic commitment to his fellows. As a friendship develops, an Australian makes and expects deeper commitments, whether these are simply understood or expressed directly.

Most Americans, on the other hand, while placing a high value on being "friendly," tend to take less seriously than Australians their relationships with, and loyalty to, particular friends, often valuing more highly a wide circle of friends. Such preferences enable Americans to move in and out of relationships more easily and more frequently than do Australians.

Consistent with their interest in limiting the depth of friendships while increasing the number of friends, Americans are careful to minimize their commitments to others. Unlike Australians, they do not necessarily expect mutual commitments to increase as familiarity increases; they are in fact, often uncomfortable if someone makes a personal commitment to them. The means by which American avoid commitments to others are numerous and subtle, and they are often confusing and disconcerting to people whose priorities are different.

Australians have traditionally expressed the priority they give to personal relationships in terms of "mateship." Through the loneliness, vast distances, and difficulties of existence experienced by the first Australians, men and women learned to help and trust each other. Australians still respect and share a genuine spirit of mateship, a sense that "we're in this thing together."

Americans seldom share this sense of mutual concern and involvement with their fellow countrymen, or even with their friends. They do sometimes approximate it in their professional relationships where they share a sense of common endeavor. The objective here, however, is not the assistance of a fellow or the developing of a relationship; rather, the objective is the accomplishment, with an associate, of a particular project or goal. The objective for American, in other words, is outside of the relationship; the relationship is valued and maintained so long as it makes possible the attainment of the external objective.

Australians therefore believe strongly that "a man's got to stick to his mate and see him through." An American is more conscious of sticking to his job and seeing his work through to completion.

This difference in priorities between Americans and Australians extends to their relations with strangers. An American will usually give assistance to a stranger, and will often give it gladly, but the American usually has to be asked for the assistance. Also, the American is likely to be concerned lest his assistance to the stranger take him too much out of his way or interrupt his schedule for too long.

An Australian, because of his priorities, is more inclined to offer assistance to a stranger. In giving this assistance, he is likely to be less concerned than the American about possible infringements upon his time.

Given their different backgrounds, values, and inclinations, Australians often feel that Americans are superficial in their relationships, especially their friendships, and they find that it is difficult to develop close, long lasting friendships with Americans.

Fellowship vs. Leadership

A related aspect of Australian culture deserves at least brief mention for it is important to Australian society and government and it illuminates some of the determinative differences between Australians and Americans. H. M. Green, an historian of Australian literature, has pointed out that "Australian conditions encourage fellowship rather than leadership." The reason for this is that Australian conditions, while encouraging homogeneity, cohesiveness, and involvement with one's fellows, have not encouraged respect for exceptional qualities.

American conditions and culture do, however, encourage the identification and reward of exceptional qualities (at least as prevailing criteria define them). The educational system recognizes certain exceptional qualities within young Americans, thereby encouraging these Americans to develop such qualities and to look for and respect such qualities in others. The mass media also make some attempt to locate and make known individuals having exceptional qualities (again, as popularly defined). Therefore Americans are conscious of, and generally appreciative of, "outstanding" persons in a variety of fields.

The implications of these differences in attitude (and therefore in perception) are many; they influence governmental, cultural, and personal relations between Australians and Americans. With regard to personal relations, one of the implications is that Americans are accustomed to being respected for (what they consider to be) their outstanding qualities--as a nation and as individuals. They are often confused, put off, and sometimes insulted when such qualities are not respected (and often not even acknowledged) by Australians. For their part, Australians feel put upon if they sense that the Americans they are with expect them to acknowledge qualities they don't look for and may not see, or show respect for qualities which they, as Australians, care little about.

Levelers vs. Achievers

Americans are quite conscious of their own status and the status of others with whom they are interacting. They define status primarily in terms of one's occupation, income, and professional position. They work at achieving status, cultivating patterns of behavior appropriate to their status, and acquiring the material goods and other symbols associated with their status. Americans are, therefore, usually willing to give at least qualified respect to someone having status.

Australians are also status-conscious. Instead of working for and respecting status, however, they are more inclined to question and even challenge it. So highly do they value egalitarianism, even more highly than do Americans, they have a strong distaste for any sign of ambition to set oneself up as superior to one's fellows. Australians are suspicious of pretention, more so than are Americans; they are critical of any affectation and they strongly resist and resent anyone who is patronizing toward them. Any attempt to "pull rank" with an Australian is resented.

These attitudes have been tested recently by the immigration into Australia of large numbers of people from the United Kingdom. The immigrants have been welcomed, but many Australians have not taken to them easily because they feel the immigrants have a sense of superiority.

Given their status-consciousness and their attitudes towards assumed superiority, Australians are alert to any pretensions when interacting with Americans and resentful when they find them. Some Australians have found that what irritates them most about Americans is their perceived attitude that "we are the best and know the most."

There are, therefore, strong leveling tendencies within Australian culture, stronger than those in American cultures. As individuals, Australians bring their leveling tendencies into numerous situations, including their interactions with Americans. When with Americans, perhaps especially in America, these tendencies are sometimes accentuated. Within the American context, tendencies sometimes become intentions.

Knowledge of One Another

The quality and content of any interaction between individuals depend, in part, upon their knowledge of one another and of their respective cultural backgrounds. Americans know very little about Australians. One reason for their ignorance is the fact that American newspapers and news magazines seldom carry articles on Australia; what articles there are usually deal with a trivial part of Australian politics or society. Australians are conscious of this, consider it negligent and regret it.

A great deal more information about America and Americans flows into Australia. Australians, therefore, assume they know much more about America. They do, in fact, know much about certain aspects to which the media give attention. Some of what they know, however, besides being only partial is also distorted, especially that which they have learned through American movies. As far as accurate knowledge about fundamental characteristics of the two cultures is concerned, especially knowledge about the significant and problem-producing differences between them, Australians know little more than do Americans.

As far as curiosity about one another's cultures is concerned, Australians often feel that they are more interested in learning about American culture than are the Americans in learning about theirs. When in the United States for a limited period of time, many Australians feel that they are rather detached from their home culture, that they are actively participating in American culture, and they want to learn and do as much as possible during their time in America. They do not feel that this kind of interest is returned. Instead, they often feel that Americans do not care about their country, cultural background, basic values and customary ways of doing things. They seldom have an opportunity to talk about Australia, which they want to do because it is their country, they care about it, and are proud of it. This in one of the reasons why interaction with Americans is not as satisfying for Australians as they would like it to be.

Impression vs. Expression

Further and more serious difficulties arise because Australians and Americans bring differing intentions, needs, and personal characteristics into their relations with one another. With regard to personal characteristics, Australian men and women are friendly, humorous, and sardonic (derisive, disdainful, and scornful). Americans are also friendly, but they are so friendly that they are seldom sardonic; they are also less humorous.

Australians have a wider range of emotional and attitudinal expression than do Americans. At one moment they can seem cordial and quite relaxed and the next voice a strong opinion or severe judgment, or take an uncompromising position. This is disconcerting for Americans who tend to place a high value upon consistency of expression and evenness of temper. Most Americans, therefore, constrict the range of their expressions, especially those Americans who spend most of their time in business, government, or academic organizations. Confronted with the fluctuations of an Australian's behavior, or even sensing the <u>possibility</u> of fluctuations, an American is apt to consider the Australian unpredictable, and therefore, not altogether reliable.

Americans need to be liked. Australians, partially because of their sometimes inconsistent behavior and sardonic manner, do not give the signals and reinforcements that tell Americans they _are_ liked. This is one of the reasons Americans often don't know where they stand with Australians.

Australians are less concerned than Americans about what others think of them; they are not as interested in whether someone likes them or not. Therefore, they do not try as hard as Americans to influence other people's opinions of them.

For Americans, if someone is similar to them, they assume that person is apt to like them. Wanting Australians to like them, Americans tend to see Australians (and others) as similar to them. Australians, although they emulate some aspects of American society, see themselves (and want to be seen by others) as _distinct_ from Americans. Therefore, while the Australian is expressing in various (perhaps rather blunt) ways that he is different from Americans, the American is hearing, "I don't like you."

Americans tend to like people who agree with them. Australians are more apt to be interested in a person who _disagrees_ with them; disagreement is a basis for a lively conversation. Similarly, Americans assume that if someone agrees with them, that person likes them; disagreement implies rejection. Australians assume that someone's disagreement with them has little to do with that person's attitude toward them. Disagreement, in fact, can indicate real interest and respect. ("The fellow cares enough to really disagree with me.") Therefore, an American usually looks for agreement from an

Australian; the Australian often responds with disagreement; the American finds he doesn't really like the Australian very much and, further, feels rejected. The Australian is puzzled, amused or perturbed.

Conscious of his status, and wanting to be liked, an American does things which he thinks will impress others. He usually does these naturally and with the expectation, based on experience with other Americans, of a favorable response. A problem arises for the American, however, when he is interacting with an Australian: it is very difficult to impress an Australian. Furthermore, Australians quickly become impatient with attempts to impress them. When asked what they find most difficult to understand about Americans, Australians sometimes reply, "Their obsession with making a 'good' impression." An American, expecting a favorable response but receiving nothing or something quite different, is left confused and disconcerted.

Occasional disharmony also occurs because Australians have strong contempt for fuss, for the finer points of protocol, and for excessive worry. Americans occasionally provoke this contempt; they can become so wrapped up in their work that they display these characteristics.

Underlying many of the points of difference and difficulty above is a difference in focus. An Australian, when trying to get a sense of a person, looks for qualities within and is especially alert to interesting personal characteristics. An American, is more apt to look at what the person does and has done. When sizing up someone in a professional setting, an Australian concentrates on the person's competence and the qualities which constitute competence. An American, in contrast, more often concentrates upon the person's accomplishments (especially the number of accomplishments), on the person's position or positions, and the number of people and the amount of money over which the person has or has had jurisdiction. Because of this difference in focus, misconnections between Australians and Americans are common; they are, however, often unrecognized.

Being more interested in personal qualities, Australians often find that the inclination of Americans to let their achievements and positions speak for them and to over-emphasize simple friendliness sometimes makes them boring. Very nice, but not very engaging or challenging. In order to evoke some definite opinions or other tangible reactions from an American, and thereby enjoy an exchange of substance and color, an Australian often becomes more self-assertive. Instead of jumping in and enjoying the exchange, however, an American is more apt to withdraw. The Australian, in response, may become more emphatic; the American then excuses himself to get another drink. "Why," Australians sometimes ask, "are Americans so afraid to show their color?"

Australians have other reasons for being assertive. One basic reason is that they tend to gain needed recognition and to develop and confirm their sense of themselves, their identity, by thinking and acting against others, against the opinions, pretensions, and expectations of others. Americans differ fundamentally here. They do, quite consistently, derive some sense of themselves by acting against their natural environment, but they increase this sense and their self-esteem by acting in accord with the actions and expectations of others. Australians and Americans, in other words, are reinforced and supported by opposite responses from other people. Therefore, when an Australian (who wants someone to push against) is with an American (who wants someone to move along with him), the Australian thinks the American is wishy-washy. The American, of course, thinks the Australian is overbearing and obnoxious.

Given these contrasts in the means through which Australians and Americans try to know and affirm themselves, it is understandable that frequently neither find their relations with the other very satisfying.

Results from research conducted by the author suggest that Australians, especially Australian men, find relationships satisfying when they are challenging. Americans, however, seem to find relationships satisfying when they are comfortable.

Trust

Given the differences outlined above, Australians and Americans trust (and distrust) persons for different reasons. An Australian tends to base his trust in a person upon the person's capacity for loyalty and commitment, and upon his own sense and estimation of the person. An American, tends to base his trust upon the person's capacity for performance and consistent behavior, and upon other people's recognition, ranking and accreditation of the person. When interacting with an American, therefore, an Australian bases his trust of the American upon his own assessment of the personal (internal) characteristics of the American. The American, however, tends to base his trust of the Australian upon the Australian's professional or role (external) characteristics. An American, therefore, is more inclined that an Australian to trust a person simply because he or she is a surgeon, baby sitter, mechanic, executive, vice-president, etc.

The different bases of trust for Australians and Americans can themselves cause distrust between the two peoples and they account, in part, for the ambivalence in the relations between them.

Respect

Closely related to this is respect. Here again there are important differences. Given their internal orientation and their sense of natural equality, Australians respect character, wherever and in whatever role it is found. Americans more often respect past and potential accomplishments, whatever the character. An Australian recognizes and respects individual worth apart from status. An American is inclined to see individual worth as derived from status, or to see status as indicative of individual worth, and therefore to assume and respect individual worth if the status is high.

The different bases of trust and respect account, in part, for the difficulty Australians and Americans have in knowing whether the other is sincere. Australians sometimes say that the most difficult thing to understand about Americans is "whether they are 'fair dinkum' or not." They wonder, "Are Americans sincere about what they say?"

Style of Conversation

In their conversation, Australians have developed and appreciate the art of deadpan understatement. Americans, who tend to take spoken words literally (except when they themselves use exaggeration and overstatement--which they do often), do not receive the full meaning and intent of Australian's understated expressions.

Australians also add a dash of cynicism to their conversation, especially when they want to counterpoint an American colleague's over-enthusiasm. Most Americans do not use cynicism and they misunderstand and are put off by it when Australians and others use it. For Americans, cynicism tends to connote a detached, judgmental attitude or anger and hostility, attitudes and feelings with which Americans are usually not comfortable, especially in face-to-face conversations. Americans, who tend to be expansive in their conversation, also have difficulty with the Australian inclination to be laconic, pithy, and pointed in conversation.

Not only do styles of conversation differ, but attitudes differ as well. Americans tend to place considerable importance upon the exact words exchanged in a conversation and upon the particular topics discussed. Certain attitudes of Australians, however, which are conveyed in the midst of conversations, suggest to Americans a general disregard for words exchanged and topics discussed. These attitudes are described by Dr. Brian Fitzpatrick, a distinguished Australian historian. He explains that, as far as Australians, especially Australian men, are concerned,

> utterance is better not done at all;
> but if it is done, when it is done,
> it were well it were slowly, flatly
> and expressionlessly, to betoken
> that the subject, any subject, is
> hardly worth talking about.

Negative Expression

Americans sometimes make negative statements about situations, conditions, and institutions. They seldom make directly negative statements about people, especially people they are with, and they are uncomfortable when others do. Australians express negative feelings and opinions about both situations and people, sometimes about people they are with. This is probably one of the reasons why some Americans have reported that the most irritating thing about Australians is that "sometimes they are brazen and sarcastic."

Americans have and often use a variety of terms conveying an objective (and therefore presumably neutral) tone, or a non-specific, non-commital positive tone. Australians, on the other hand, use hundreds of casual, colorful terms to suggest a tone of amiable, tolerant contempt. Americans taking such terms out of their Australian context and interpreting them as if an American had used them, are apt to see Australians as crude, critical and conceited. Also aware of Australian's inclinations to be personally evaluative and to express negative reactions, Americans are often vaguely uneasy; concerned lest the Australians apply their scrutiny and negative evaluations directly to them.

Humor

Both Australians and Americans enjoy and appreciate humor, especially informal, spontaneous humor. Australians, however, feel that humor is appropriate (and even essential) in a wider variety of situations than do Americans. Also Australians bring some of their cynicism into their humor. The result is that Americans sometimes feel that Australians' humor is out of place or is disrespectful, harsh and offensive. Australians, in turn, tend to feel that Americans are too serious, too heavy, and that the humor of Americans is too constrained and lacking in color and spice. This results in each having some difficulty understanding and responding to the humor of the other. There is evidence that Australian women have special difficulty with American humor, more than do Australian men.

Fundamental differences between two peoples are often revealed when they are under stress. An American, when he is working under stress, rolls up his sleeves, "digs in," concentrating more intensely and becoming more serious. An Australian under stress, tends to jest and tries to lighten things up a bit (while, of course, continuing to do his work). As the pressure increases, the American bears down harder; the Australian sees more and says more that is ironic and funny. At those very points that the American expects seriousness and total attention to the task at hand, the Australian leans back and tosses off a clever quip.

Consistency and Contradiction

Because they prefer consistency and predictability, and are accustomed to role-conformity (and therefore consistent) behavior, Americans are reluctant to accept contradictions either within themselves and their own behavior or within others and their behavior. This preference poses a problem for Americans when they are interacting with Australians because Australians are usually not bothered by contradictions. Sometimes, in fact, they are interested in them and respectful of them. Furthermore, Australians are themselves often contradictory.

An Australian, for example, has no objection to some humor mixed in with his serious concerns (politics would be one of them), nor does he object to some grimness mixed with his jests. An American, by predisposition, separates the important (and therefore, in his mind, the serious) from the playful.

There are further causes of confusion for Americans. Australians are boastful but also highly self-critical. They enjoy living for the day but can also be gloomily introspective. They are a life-embracing people who have imposed upon their instinct for enjoyment a spirit and a social policy of denial. They have a deeply-rooted exuberance but have imposed upon themselves severe restraints. They drink heavily, for example, but follow policies of temperance (hours for drinking, for instance, are limited as are the locations--primarily bars inside hotels).

Australians also show both rashness and prudence. They have a penchant for cool, extravagant gambling (lotteries, horse racing, and the national game of "two-up"). At the same time, they save more money per capita than most other people in the world. Saving banks are proliferating in Australia, life insurance is widely held, and many Australians are determined to own their own house surrounded by a carefully tended garden.

Due to their environment and their experiences during the early decades on their continent, Australians have long felt lonely. The creations of their contemporary painters reveal that their inner loneliness persists. Americans sometimes sense this, yet Americans see at the same time Australian attitudes and behavior which, to them, hardly seem calculated to earn respect, establish rapport, develop friendly relations, and thereby overcome some of this loneliness.

Such contradictions are disturbing for Americans. They tend to see situations and people in terms of "either-or," and they are uncomfortable when they can't. They tend to classify their relationships in the same way: "either he likes me or he doesn't;" then they determine their response accordingly. Confronted with contradictions as they are when interacting with Australians, Americans often maintain some distance and respond with some ambivalence. Americans have said that the

most difficult thing for them to understand about Australians
is "What really is behind their actions," and "What do they
really think."

Some Suggestions for Americans

As is clear from the analysis up to this point in the
study, Americans and Australians often have difficulty getting
along comfortably and enjoyably with one another. Informed,
conscientious effort on the part of both, however, can increase
considerably their mutual satisfaction. Specific steps both
can take are implicit in the sections above. Some of the
constructive steps Americans can take will be suggested here.

- Show genuine interest in Australia. Learn about the
  land, the traditions, and the society which have shaped
  so profoundly the values, priorities, and expectations
  of Australians today. Find out enough, through
  reading and conversation, to ask intelligent questions
  and make perceptive observations about Australians and
  their unique country.

- Do not be misled by the superficial similarities
  between Australians and Americans (language, skin
  color, dress, etc.). Anticipate and recognize the
  significant differences. Know exactly the points at
  which misunderstanding and tension are likely to
  occur. Make clear to other Americans the consequences
  of assuming that Australians are pretty much like most
  Americans. That assumption, itself, will antagonize
  the Australian.

- Initiate social (and business) activities for Australians and Americans which provide opportunities for <u>cooperative</u> effort, activities which involve everyone on an equal basis.

- Set aside your symbols of status--your title, connections, accomplishments, possessions--and simply present the Australian with yourself: your idiosyncrasies, prejudices, wit, curiosity, concerns, frustrations, hopes, etc.

- Stand ready, in a relaxed manner, to be tested. The Australian may challenge you and probe to see if you are a person of substance, someone with a backbone, some steel inside, some depth and character.

- Practice testing and sparring with the Australian yourself.

- Make up your own mind about the Australian, regardless of what others have said about the person. Regardless, too, of what the Australian says about himself. He will be making up his mind while sparring with you.

- Recognize and appreciate the strength and complexity of character in the Australian. Don't be distracted by external matters (his rank and influence, for example, or his lack of these).

- When talking with an Australian, take a definite position. Let him (or her) know where you stand, what you believe, what you feel. Show disconcernment, make judgements regarding people and events, express strong opinions (if, of course, they are genuine). Do this briefly and emphatically--and usually quietly. In other words, give the Australian a sense of who you are as a person. Give him something to react to.

- Do not depend upon an Australian to like you. Don't try to do things and say things you think will make him like you. It won't work. If you need to be liked, be sure to spend some time with others who, themselves, need to be liked.

- Do not expect the Australians around you to regard you as outstanding (because of your achievements, power, stature in the community, etc.). In their eyes you probably are not outstanding, but that doesn't matter much to them. If you begin to intentionally display some of the exceptional qualities which may have made you "outstanding," you may soon wish you hadn't.

- Do not try to out-do an Australian or prove to him you are better at something. If in fact you are, he will know it. If you don't try to prove it, he will respect your ability.

- Do not say something unless you mean it. An Australian will respect and respond to sincerity. Any hint of something phony, any pretense, will quickly turn him off.

- Use _few_ words, choose them carefully but say them casually. Practice conveying much of your meaning through your intonation, rather than simply adding more and more words.

- Allow room for Australians (and others) to behave in (what seems to be) contradictory, unpredictable ways. Enjoy it.

- Accept the fact that conversations do not have to be "pleasant" and "flow smoothly." Figure out more ways to make yours engaging, colorful, stimulating.

- Develop personal resilience. Don't be put off by derisive comments, undercutting, and cynicism. Don't disagree with a critical remark simply to smooth things over. Don't agree simply to avoid an argument. Give _your_ _own_ judgment on the matter, whatever your judgment is.

- Do not feel rejected when an Australian disagrees with you, even if he (or she) does so categorically and vehemently. Enjoy the debate, spice it with some wit and some pithy thrusts, meanwhile listening for the Australians' intentions and intriguing qualities, not just his words.

- When uncomfortable with an Australian, don't revert to formality. Keep the exchanges informal, direct and to the point.

- Self-deprecating humor is often helpful (especially because Australians often feel many Americans consider themselves to be the best at everything and they really resent such assumptions of superiority).

- Don't be patronizing toward an Australian. Don't try to protect him (or her). Care about him, pitch in to help him, but don't sympathize with him, don't coddle or soothe him, and don't in any way try to be take care of him. He is fully able to take care of himself (as he will be quick to let you know).

- Do not pretend to more camaraderie or friendship with an Australian than you actually feel. Don't try to be "good friends" with many Australians. Choose one or two. If you want a close friendship with an Australian, be prepared to commit a fair amount of yourself to the relationship, and look forward to receiving a lot in return.

These steps do not guarantee constructive relations between Australians and Americans. Their differences are deep; their antagonisms can be severe. If the American takes these steps, however, and if the Australian meets him part way, the chances are much higher that they will overcome their ambivalence and be able to enjoy a mutually satisfying relationship.

Bludgers vs. Producers

Looking specifically now at differences and sources of difficulty within an organizational context, we find significant differences in Australians and American attitudes toward work itself. Some say that an Australian considers work to be a bloody nuisance and therefore does as little of it as slowly as he can. Australians do have only qualified respect for hard work and are reluctant to expend effort on any kind of unnecessary activity (such as, in A. L. McLeod's words, "standing up straight if there is a handy post to lean on"). They have some of the shortest working hours in the world and during them stop frequently to enjoy their "smoke-ohs."

"An Australian becomes aware at an early age that work is a national joke," explains Robert Haupt, Washington correspondent for the Australian Financial Review. He goes on, "People who work hard are as likely to attract suspicion as praise, while a whole folklore surrounds the 'bludger'." (A bludger is that person, much admired, who has perfected the art of appearing to do a prodigious amount of work while actually doing very little.)

Throughout their history, of course, Americans have felt very differently about their work. The long hours at the office, the stuffed brief case lugged home each evening, the pressure and the overtime to meet the critical deadline, the President who puts in two hours each morning before anyone else arrives, are characteristic patterns of American working life. While such "dedication" and exertion is often not enjoyed, and even regretted, it is still respected and certainly considered when decisions on promotion are being made.

Because of this conscientiousness in their work, Americans often see Australians as lacking commitment where it counts, lacking self-discipline, and therefore probably unreliable in the crunch. Americans believe deeply that they can do anything if they work hard enought at it. Australians tend to feel that they can probably do anything, but that the effort required to do it will probably be minimal.

Given these differences, there is evidence from our research that the attitudes of Australians toward work do begin to change while they are working in the United States with Americans, provided they are in the country for an extended period of time.

Inner-Directed vs. Other Directed

A fundamental distinction affecting their relations on he job (and elsewhere) is that Australians tend to be inner-directed whereas Americans are usually quite other-directed. An Australian often bases his evaluations and behavior upon things inside himself--his own feelings, preferences, and expectations. An American is more apt to base his evaluations and behavior on things outside of himself--corporate policy, the particular situation, or other people's behavior and their expectations.

The conflict between those who are inner-directed and those who are other-directed can be especially noticeable in an organizational context. An American is usually more willing to conform to the structure, roles, and norms of an organization. An Australian is more apt to take organizational structure, roles, and norms more lightly and move quite easily outside of them (or against them). In addition, Americans expect conformity from others, including Australians. Australians, however, are inclined to resist these expectations. The American then puts some pressure on the Australian to conform; the Australian resists more firmly. The Australian begins to see the American as critical and pretentious; the American sees the Australian as uncooperative and obstinate.

Because Australians are more inner-directed than Americans, they usually do not shift their approach, behavior, and expectations depending upon the class, status, and culture (factors external to the Australian) of those with whom they are interacting. Americans place some value on social adaptability and are somewhat more willing and better able to make these kinds of shifts. Therefore, Americans, noticing Australians' reluctance to conform and to adjust to differences of class and status, often feel Australians are self-centered, disrepectful, and intolerant. Working with Australians can, as a result, be frustrating and irritating for Americans.

Problems arising from an internal as opposed to an external locus of evaluation and action are increasing in severity in American culture. As policies, procedures, and performance in industrial organizations become more standarized, and as the organizations struggle more intensely to keep a competitive edge, the Americans in them may become less tolerant of those who don't "toe the line." In the midst of difficult economic conditions, Americans have become even less tolerant of those who don't fit--especially those who won't fit. Asians don't fit but will. Australians don't fit and won't.

The differences above are some of the reasons why Americans sometimes indicate that they would prefer to spend time, both socially and professionally, with Asians rather than Australians.

Measuring Up To Standards

As is evident in the above, attitudes toward specific standards differ significantly. Australians, given their more internal orientation, tend to be rather indifferent toward standards (standards being external guides to decision and action). Whether a person's performance or a product meets a particular standard is, therefore, not of great concern to an Australian. When questioned about it, he is apt to respond simply, "She'll do" or "She'll be right, mate."

Americans, on the other hand, because of their more external orientation, their educational or organization procedures, and more recently because of governmental regulations, are very conscious of standards. While they may not be as concerned as they used to be about standards of quality, they are still much concerned about standards of efficiency, productivity, and profitability.

Given their differing respect for standards, Australians sometimes see Americans as driven, restricted (and restricting) nit-pickers. Americans sometimes see Australians as negligent and sloppy.

Laws and regulations are set up with the same basic intent as standards (namely, to induce conformity), and they often evoke the same kind of response. Australians tend not to like them. One of the most noticeable differences revealed by our research was that <u>relaxed</u> laws and regulations are considerably more important to the Australians' motivation to work carefully and productively than they are to the Americans' motivation.

The differences between Australians and Americans in their attitudes toward work and standards make it difficult for each to understand and do what the other expects. Australian men, especially, have difficulty knowing what American friends and co-workers expect. When working in the United States, they usually experience some role shock.

Authority

Australians are, generally speaking, disrespectful of authority (a fundamental reason being that it claims to be an external guide to decision and action). Americans, however, are inclined to accept limited authority over them, abide by it, and even acquire it for themselves. These contrasting attitudes are the source of much of the friction and irritation often experienced by Australians and Americans when they are trying to work together.

The Australians' resentment of superiors, like their loyalty to equals, is deeply rooted and long standing. It had its origins in their early experience in the outback and was reinforced by the bush ethos, the bush unions, and the <u>Bulletin</u> (a widely circulated and influential nationalist weekly published in Sidney around the turn of the century). Their resentment has now become a consistent cultural theme.

Americans, from their earliest decades, have designed their structures of authority very carefully. During this century particular attention has been given to the structures of authority in government and business organizations, for these structures give American society some of its stability and continuity. These have become especially important during recent decades as the authority of the family and of ethnic and religious communities have been disintegrating. Americans, therefore, tend to respect prevalent structures of authority; Americans are accustomed to them and need them for a predictable framework within which to function.

Australian's strong preference for a relaxed, open style carries over into their working relationships, making them more informal than Americans in organizational contexts. Australians' deep feeling for democratic equality also carries over, making possible for employees a lack of deference in their dealings with employers. An American, however, expects some deference from those "beneath" him. When working with Americans, Australians seldom feel or show this deference.

Consequently, an Australian does not easily accept a hierarchy, a particular station, or defined duties associated with that station. It is because he must still work within some hierarchies and regulations that the Australian sustains within his imagination the land and the life-style of the country; it provides for him a sense of space and a needed release from the restrictions, conventions, and routine of his life within the confines of the city and the organizations. Americans are more comfortable within a hierarchy. An American likes his role and status more clearly defined and is usually willing to give a higher position the respect deemed appropriate to it.

Although Australians are not altogether comfortable when located within a hierarchy and are not by nature respectful of superiors, their relations with their employers and supervisors are definitely important to them. The results of our research suggest that, although interpersonal relations with co-workers are important to the motivation of both Australians and Americans, interpersonal relations with <u>supervisors</u> are more important to Australians (than Americans) if they are to work carefully and productively. (Illustrating further the importance of relationships to Australians, this research suggests that the encouragement of one's spouse is also more important to an Australian's motivation to work carefully and productively than it is to an American's.)

Related to authority and supervision is accountability--a central feature in American business and industry. Whereas Americans accept and insist upon accountability, Australians regard it with some reservations and can be much bothered by it.

Control is also an essential factor in considerations of authority. Americans are usually more conscious of, and concerned about control than are Australians. It is becoming increasingly important to Americans, especially American managers, because of the characteristically intense competition among individuals, groups, and institutions for control, because of the increasing complexity of managerial tasks, and because Americans are becoming increasingly aware that much upon which they depend is now beyond their control (the environment, basic resources, the international economy, etc.). Control over personnel, among other factors of production, is therefore being given more careful attention. Australian personnel, of course, resist and resent being controlled.

As was true with regard to trust and respect, an Australian will accept authority and control over him (albeit reluctantly) if he considers the person exercising authority to be competent and interesting--to have, in other words, acceptable personal qualities. An American's acceptance is based more upon the particular position and the amount of authority associated with it (and probably some thought as to where compliance will get him).

It is the concern of Americans for status, hierarchy, deference, and positions of authority that sometimes give Australians the feeling that they cannot relate directly with Americans. One Australian working in the United States, for example, explained that the most irritating thing about Americans for him was "their reluctance to lower their guard, to just be themselves."

For a clear example of Australian attitudes toward authority, control and obedience, it is helpful to look again at the Australian digger in France during the First World War. Dr. C. W. Bean explains that,

> . . .at heart even the oldest Australian soldier was incorrigibly civilian. However thoroughly he accepted the rigid army methods as conditions temporarily necessary, he never became reconciled to continuous obedience to orders, existence by rule and lack of privacy. His individualism had been so strongly implanted as to stand out after years of subordination.

Instead of obeying, an Australian is more accustomed to bargaining. When handed, or more often sent, instructions from an American, his sense of equality and fellowship is violated and his response is resistance. If approached more personally and as an equal with experience and opinions worthy of consideration, he may be more inclined to engage and bargain; negotiation and cooperation might then become the mode of interaction, rather than argument and resentment.

Decision-Making

Many of the basic differences described above and in the following also imply significant differences in preferred procedures for making decisions. One particular difference was suggested in the results of our research. Australians are quite collaborative in their orientation. They believe quite strongly that decision-making procedures should be based upon management's assumption that subordinates share equal interests, organizational goals, and success; they should be consulted on major organizational decisions in order to reach a total organizational consensus.

Americans, however, are somewhat less collaborative. They are inclined to believe that subordinates have less to contribute to organizational decisions and less right to make demands on management or the organization.

Motivation

Because Americans value so highly accomplishments and achievements and derive much of their self-esteem from them, Americans are strongly motivated by the prospect of achievement. Complementing this, Americans are professionally highly ambitious. They expend considerable energy, sometimes exhausting themselves, in trying to realize their ambitions, achieve status and position, and obtain wealth and honors. Australians in contrast, are not so eager to excel and tend to distrust prestigious positions, wealth, and honors.

While Australians usually appreciate the industriousness of Americans, they are put off by their excessive exertion. Some Australians, for example, when asked what they found most difficult to understand about Americans, have responded, "Their drive and push in business," and "Complete dedication to the 'rat race' and making money."

Achievement and position are often symbolized for Americans by the level of their salary. Consistent with this, salary provides more motivation for Americans to work carefully and productively than it does for Australians.

Americans are also motivated by the challenge and involvement of particular tasks, projects, the work itself. Being quite task-oriented, they tend to concentrate exclusively on the task at hand. Australians, although they are usually concerned about the task at hand, are often at the same time aware of their own more personal interests and the particular personalities of the others working on the task.

In that tasks are accomplished and goals are achieved in the future, Americans tend still to be quite future-oriented. Planning, for example, is a major preoccupation of the American and a fundamental function of American organizations. Australians are more interested in the present, less anxious about the details of planning and less willing to postpone satisfaction and enjoyment until some later time. An American who has worked with Australians, for example, finds that the most difficult thing to understand about Australians is that "they seem to live only for today."

Seeing or at least sensing these differences in Australians, an American is likely to view an Australian as uninvolved and even careless in his work. An Australian, sensing the differences, is apt to see an American as uninvolved and careless in his relationships and a captive of the future.

Taking Risk

Americans sometimes also see Australians as lacking care in their work and seriousness in their purpose because Australians, consistent with their aggressive gambling inclinations, are more willing to take risks.

Traditionally, American business and industry and Americans themselves have ventured with enthusiasm into situations involving risk, even great risk. During recent decades, however, corporations in most sectors have become more cautious and more concerned about self-perpetuation and steady, predictable growth. Individuals may have become more conforming and more concerned about job-security, acceptance, and predictable advancement. Americans are, therefore, sometimes uneasy working with Australians for Australians stand ready "to have a go at a thing."

Giving Credit

Australians, because of their egalitarian spirit, are reluctant to give anyone credit. Even in the case of a person with extraordinary competence and an engaging manner, Australians, while appreciating these qualities, will seldom acknowledge or commend them directly and publicly. Australians are especially reluctant to give Americans credit because Americans expect it and, in the Australians' view, already think too highly of themselves.

Pace of Life

In both their social and work relations, Australians (like representatives of many other cultures) have difficulties with the pace of life maintained by most Americans. Essentially and deliberately easy-going themselves, Australians often feel pushed and pressured while living in the United States. Australian women, especially, have difficulties adjusting to the hectic pace of American life.

On the job in the United States, Australians experience a conflict. They want to do a good job and, with reservations, want to meet the expectations others place upon them; to do so, however, requires a pace which is too demanding, abrasive, and personally debilitating. Their response, therefore, is dissatisfaction, resistance, criticism, and resentment. The pace is especially difficult for Australians to accept and keep up with if their assignments in the United States are short; they tend to view such assignments as something of a vacation.

In the course of our research, we asked Australians working in the United States, "What characteristic of your own culture would most be beneficial for Americans if they were to adopt it for themselves in their lives here in America?" An Australian man represented the feelings of many Australians when he replied, "To slow down the rush and enjoy life."

Conflict

Given the above differences between Australians and Americans, in both their social and work relations, as well as some of the similarities between them, they are sometimes in conflict with one another. Such conflict may be intensified because of a further (and fundamental) difference: their experience with and attitudes toward conflict itself.

Americans do not like conflict, especially interpersonal conflict. They are uncomfortable in the midst of it and concerned about others' opinions of them after having engaged in it. Americans are, therefore, inclined and even determined to avoid being involved in direct conflict themselves and they have a variety of means (personal, legal, and organizational) for doing so.

Australians, however, tend not to mind conflict and, in fact, sometimes enjoy it, intentionally engage in it, and even respect others who carry it off with style and results. Australians are more accustomed to conflict and more resilient in the midst of it. They are also less concerned about negative reactions from those with whom they come into conflict.

Differing attitudes toward conflict become additional sources for contrasting expectations, negative feelings, and further difficulties between Australians and Americans.

Suggestions for Americans on the Job

Relations between the two peoples we are considering can usually be made more productive if both are conscious of their different values and preferences described above, and if each learns to do certain things which the other will respect and enjoy. Many of the appropriate things an American can do are implied in the previous sections. Some are suggested more explicitly below.

- Negotiate with an Australian, don't issue orders to him (or her). Collaborate, don't compete. Take participative management seriously and practice it consistently.

- Integrate with your task orientation a genuine, day-to-day person orientation. Be as interested in personality as productivity.

- If you are supervising an Australian, pay particular attention to your personal relationship with him. The quality of your relationship will influence his motivation and his performance.

- Be easily accessible, regardless of how high your position.

- An Australian working for you considers himself your equal in every way that matters to him. Treat him as a person having real substance and worthy opinions.

- Do not expect deference from an Australian who is working with you. Don't give him deference if you are working for him.

- Keep the structure of your organization as loose and open as possible. Rigidity often results in resentment.

- Keep rules, regulations, and other requirements for conformity to a minimum.

- Standards of performance and other formal (as well as informal) expectations must, of course, be reasonable and must be very clear and acceptable to the Australians who must meet them.

- Keep procedures which monitor, measure, and control efficiency and performance of personnel to a minimum.

- Push yourself as hard and log as much overtime as you like, but don't expect Australians to follow suit. Time on and guaranteed time off must be agreed upon at the outset. Job assignments, work schedules, and work loads must take into account the Australian's preferences and priorities and should be worked out directly with him. He may be willing to carry a lot of responsibility but he will have things other than work which he fully intends to do.

- The pace at which an Australian is most productive is usually slightly faster than the one at which he is accustomed to working in an Australian organization in his own country. To insist that he work at a much more rapid pace and meet even more pressing deadlines (as many Americans are inclined to do) will frustrate and irritate him and simply reduce his efficiency.

- To determine the depth of an Australian's commitment to a project or a person, or the seriousness with which he takes a particular assignment, pay attention to what he does about it, and where he does it, not so much what he says about it.

- Continue making projections and planning for tomorrow, but don't be preoccupied with the future. Take full advantage of today; enjoy being with your people today.

- When discussing business matters with an Australian, don't spend a lot of time on peripheral details, fine points of interpretation, splitting hairs to make a point. Stick to matters of substance, the major issues, and be done with it.

- If you have taken a particular position on an issue which an Australian rejects, don't feel you must continually defend yourself. State your reasons clearly, very concisely, and move on.

- Do not expect sympathy, compliments, or positive feedback from an Australian. You probably won't get them, especially if you do expect them. Don't overdo positive feedback to the Australian; a few words or a gesture at the most.

- If you are going to criticize an Australian, do it directly and with some respect. Don't beat around the bush, don't pussyfoot. Also, of course, be certain the criticism is necessary and justified. If it isn't, you (and others) will certainly hear about it. Australians, unlike people from some other cultures, will fight you point by point if they feel your criticism is not justified.

- Don't hide from Australians behind your status, "heavy workload," technical jargon, or superficial chitchat. Deal directly with them.

- Prevent interpersonal conflicts with Australians. They are difficult to resolve. If one develops, however, don't avoid it. Having prepared for such conflicts (in part through understanding the Australian's values and point-of-view), walk into it, practice various ways of seeing it through with satisfactory results, and enjoy it. And don't worry about what the Australian may be thinking about you in the midst of the conflict or afterwards. He won't be worried about what you may think of him.

- If you start becoming officious or presumptious, expect to be knocked down. If by chance the Australian is being presumptious, try bringing him down a few pegs. He may be amused and may respect you for it.

- Do not try to cover up your mistakes. Don't dwell on them either. Own up to them--briefly and with a touch of humor--then move on.

- By all means party with the Australians. Loosen up, let go a bit. Don't make any appointments for early the next morning.

Many of these guidelines, of course, are appropriate when working with Americans. They are especially important, however, when working with Australians.

Common Conditions and Possibilities

The latter part of the twentieth century finds the peoples of both Australia and America uncertain and dissatisfied. Both lack central, integrating, motivating ideas adequate to their present needs and both lack a sense of common purpose and direction as they move into the next decades. Both are vulnerable, more vulnerable then either would like to be.

Among Australians there is an increasing feeling that the Bush Legend and the concepts associated with mateship, though still respected, are no longer sufficient for their highly industrialized country and thoroughly urbanized lives. Some Australians search for substitutes, many debate contemporary values, but no appropriate substitutes have yet been found.

Australians today are not much concerned with their origins. Instead, although they are not ones to worry excessively about who they are, they are more concerned about finding and maintaining their distinctive identity.

While they are reflective, forthright, and full of character as individuals, Australians are also concerned about their collective, national life, especially their politics; this, they feel, is often unimaginative, drab, sterile, complacent, and mediocre.

Related to their sense of identity and the quality of their national life are their difficulties with things American. Australians respect and depend upon the products and techniques of America. They find such things so attractive, in fact, that their distinguished architect, Robin Boyd, has coined the term "Austerican" to describe his people's susceptibility to these superficial manifestations of American culture. On the other hand, Australians are severely critical of the material basis of American culture. Furthermore, they would like to see themselves, and actually be, quite independent, self-initiating, and self-sufficient. The fact of their susceptibility and dependence causes confusion and resentment.

Given their cultural, technological, and economic dependence upon America, and upon many other countries as well, Australians are beginning to realize their vulnerability. They do not anticipate catastrophe. Australians have always had little sense of tragedy. But they do doubt increasingly the value, stability, and direction of their culture.

Americans, too, have doubts about their own culture. The American ideal that every man makes and remakes himself is no longer compelling or even real. Americans are beginning to realize that there may be no more second chances. Self-reliance, though still wished for, is no longer possible. Individual Americans, unable to provide for themselves even their basic necessities (food, clothing, housing, health, transportation, etc.), must now rely almost completely upon conglomerates, bureaucrats, experts, and repairmen.

Progress, as a priority, is still valued by Americans, though now with some dissatisfaction; it has not provided all that they once expected it to. Increasing consumption, Americans have found, leaves them wanting something more. Expansion, success, achievement, developing still another frontier, may no longer be feasible, they feel; it may not even be desirable. Technological advance and economic growth have their costs; perhaps they should be limited.

During the last decade, especially, Americans have experienced shocks to their confidence and self-esteem. Being externally oriented, Americans have been forced by a series of disconcerting events to discard some of their most sustaining illusions. Among these are their illusions regarding their inexhaustable resources and their military and moral superiority. They have recognized their own capacities for corruption and destruction.

Among Americans today, therefore, there is some sense of discouragement. There is also a sense of alienation--from nature, institutions, different generations, from themselves. And there is a sense of bewilderment; traditional priorities are being strongly challenged, values are much in flux, and major projects seem so complex as to confound even the experts and deny any satisfactory solution. These prevailing conditions, together with American's more tangible recognition of their dependence upon others whom they don't know and are not sure they can trust, have given Americans a sense of uncertainty and vulnerability.

Like Australians, therefore, Americans are searching and debating. They, too, are in need of a new integrating, motivating sense of purpose and direction, and compelling ideas suitable to the modern age. Also like the Australians, contemporary Americans have yet to find their center.

Because they both face these dilemmas, Australians and Americans are in need of assistance from one another. Because as people they differ significantly from one another, they are in advantageous positions to provide this assistance; they can suggest to one another the most valuable kinds of perspectives and alternatives. They can provide such assistance, and they can work more enjoyably and productively together, if they perceive more deeply and accurately both their similarities and their differences.

Opportunities for doing so will be numerous. Contacts between Australians and Americans will undoubtedly increase during the coming decades. Americans will be working in Australia, as they are now, often in subsidiaries of U.S. companies. Australians will be in the United States on short and long-term assignments. Increasing numbers of people from both countries will be involved in joint projects in third countries, especially in Asia.

If these two peoples who differ on such fundamental points are to get along better with one another and work together with more satisfaction, both must give up their illusion that they are quite similar to one another. Both must begin to investigate their differences, learn to <u>take</u> <u>advantage</u> of these, and act in ways more congenial to the other.

REFERENCES

Alexander, Fred. Australia and the United States. World
  Peace Foundation, Boston, 1941

Clark, Alfred W. and Sue McCabe "Leadership Beliefs of
  Australian Managers," Journal of Applied Psychology.
  Vol. 54, No. 1, Part 1, February, 1970

Crawford, R. M. Australia. Hutchinson University Library,
  London, 1970

Greenway, John. Australia: The Last Frontier. Dodd, Mead
  and Company, New York, 1972

Horne, Donald. The Australian People: Biography of a
  Nation. Angus and Robertson, 1972

Learmonth, Nancy. The Australians: How They Live and
  Work. Praeger Publishers, New York, 1973

McLeod, A. L., ed. The Pattern of Australian Culture.
  Cornell University Press, Ithaca, New York, 1963

MacInnes, Colin. Australia and New Zealand. Life World
  Library, Time, Inc., New York, 1964

Renwick, George W. Research and Evaluation of
  Cross-Cultural Training Programs Involving Australians
  and Americans. Unpublished in-house reports 1975-1980

Ward, Russel. Australia. Prentice-Hall, Inc., Englewood
  Cliffs, New Jersey, 1965

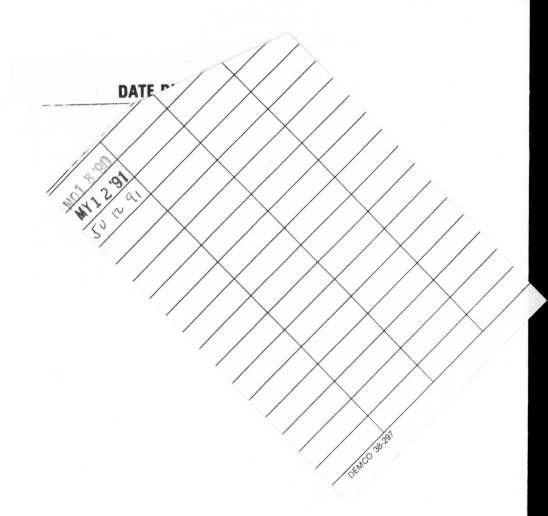

DATE D

NO1 8 '90

MY 1 2 '91

JU 12 91

DEMCO 38-297